FRENCH FOR ALL

AN EASY GUIDE TO FRENCH GRAMMAR

BEJAN IRANI

Copyright © Bejan Irani
All Rights Reserved.

ISBN 979-888546645-5

This book has been published with all efforts taken to make the material error-free after the consent of the author. However, the author and the publisher do not assume and hereby disclaim any liability to any party for any loss, damage, or disruption caused by errors or omissions, whether such errors or omissions result from negligence, accident, or any other cause.

While every effort has been made to avoid any mistake or omission, this publication is being sold on the condition and understanding that neither the author nor the publishers or printers would be liable in any manner to any person by reason of any mistake or omission in this publication or for any action taken or omitted to be taken or advice rendered or accepted on the basis of this work. For any defect in printing or binding the publishers will be liable only to replace the defective copy by another copy of this work then available.

I would like to dedicate this book to all my revered spiritual masters who have guided me in living a life based on the maxim, ***"simple life and think high."***

Next I dedicate this book to all the students who are facing difficulties in understanding and applying the French grammar taught at school.

It is very easy to understand but because of having so many subjects to study at school level children don't have time to focus on French and thereby, score less marks.

Contents

Foreword vii

Acknowledgements ix

1. Nouns (les Noms) — 1
2. Les Articles (the Articles) — 3
3. Les Adjectifs — 8
4. Adjectives Possessifs: — 17
5. Adjectives Démonstratives — 19
6. Verbs — 21
7. The Big Five Verbs (five Important Verbs) — 26
8. Pronominal Verbs (reflexive Verbs) — 29
9. Irregular Verbs — 31
10. Les Expressions Negatifs — 34
11. Le Comparatif Et Superlatif — 36
12. Les Pronoms Objets — 39
13. Tenses - Passé Composé — 51
14. Tenses - Futur Proche Et Passé Récent — 56
15. Tenses - Futur Simple — 58
16. Tenses - Imparfait — 61
17. Tenses - Plus Que Parfait (pqp) — 63
18. Tenses - Futur Antèrieur — 64
19. Nominalisation (noun Forms) — 65
20. Subjontif — 68
21. Discour Rapporté — 72
22. Present Participle And Grondif — 74
23. Conditionnel (présent Et Pass) — 76

Note To The Reader — 79

Foreword

Bejan Irani a French lingual teacher and tutor, celebrates a stellar name and career amongst some the finest academic institutions, across counties and continents.

I've had the pleasure of knowing him personally and have seen him eloquently simplify the teaching and tutoring so that almost anyone can grasp, comprehend and become proficient in reading, writing and speaking French.

Bejan is an expert in this field, be you a beginner, an intermediate or veteran you will amass a volume of understanding and application to help you achieve next level success in your French education and communication.

- Vinesh Maharaj
International Motivational Speaker

Acknowledgements

I would like to thank all the fellow teachers who have always inspred me to do my best to serve the student community. Special thanks to my spiritual master HH Kadamba Kanana Swami who indirectly asked me to take up to this profession where I can be of some help to the students in making their life well grommed when it comes to learning and mastering a foreign language.

I thank Kamala Devi who has always been encouraging me to write this book for the assistance and betterment of the students. Thanks also to my sister Madhumati Devi by who's inspiration I learnt this beautiful language that I am now sharing it with the world especially the student community.

Last but not the least i wouls like to thanks my french teachers' team at Vibgyor High, Magarpatta by whose help I could make this possible. Special thanks to Priyanka Swami who edited this book thereby redding it of its faults.

CHAPTER ONE

Nouns (Les noms)

As in every language French too has nouns. A noun is commonly defined as a person, place, or thing.

Gender: In French, all nouns have a gender i.e. masculine and feminine. It is absolutely essential to learn the gender of a noun at the same time. They are always preceded by an article. The best way to learn the noun is by learning an article with every noun, rather than just the noun itself.

We can make the nouns plural by the following methods:

1. By adding a "s"

   Like in English most nouns follow this rule.
   Ex: stylo – stylos
   crayon – crayons, etc.

2. The nouns ending in "x", "s" and "z" do not change in plural.

   Ex: prix – prix
   bas – bas
   nez – nez, etc.

3. Nouns ending in "eu", "eau", "al" will take a "x" at the end.

   Ex: gateau – gateaux

jeu - jeux
animal – animaux, etc.

CHAPTER TWO

LES ARTICLES (THE ARTICLES)

Unlike English in French it is obligatory/ compulsory to use articles for every noun.

All the nouns are divided either into masculine or feminine and they should be preceded by an article.

There are in all four types of articles. They are as follows.

1. Les articles indefinis (indefinite articles)
2. Les articles definis (definite articles)
3. Les articles contractés (contracted articles)
4. Les articles partitifs (partitive articles)

What follows is an easy to understand explanation of all the above with examples.

1. **Les articles indefinis (indefinite articles):**

These are indefinite articles which are also used in the English language denoting "a", "an" and "some". Generally used to point out things that are not specific. E.g. – a book, an eraser etc.

In French they are as follows:
Un – a/an (masculine) ex. un garçon – a boy
Un stylo – a pen, un avion – an airplane.

Une – a/an (feminine) ex. une fille – a girl
Une gomme – an eraser, une règle – a rule.
Des – some (plural) – ex. des garcons – (some)boys
Des filles – (some)girl.
When we use them in a sentence they are as follows:
Singular - Je suis un garcon. – I am a boy.
Plural - Nous sommes des garcons. – we are (some) boys.
Singular - Martina est une fille. – Martina is a girl.
Plural - Martina et Christine sont des filles. - Martina and Christine are (some) girls.

2. **Les articles definis (definite articles) :**

Unlike the indefinite articles, these point out specific nouns and used in English as "the".
E.g. – the boys, the girls, the pens etc.
In French they are as follows:
Le – the (masculine) ex. le garçon – the boy, le stylo – the pen, etc.
La – the (feminine) ex. une fille – the girl, la gomme – the eraser, la règle – the ruler etc.
L' – the (used before vowels) – ex. l'avion – the airplane, l'homme – the man etc.
Les – the (plural) – ex. les garcons – the boys, les filles – the girls, les homes – the men etc.
When we use them in a sentence they are as follows:
Singular - C'est le stylo – This is the pen.
Plural - Ce sont les stylos – These are the pens.
Singular - Martina est la fille du directeur. – Martina is the girl daughter of the director.
Plural - Martina et Christine sont les filles de classe 10. - Martina and Christine are the girls of 10th class.
Singular - C'est l'avion d'Air France. – This is the plane of Air France.

Plural - Ce sont les avions d'Air Canada. – These are the planes of Air Canada.

3. **Les articles contractés (contracted articles):**

   These are used in combination of the prepositions:
   à – to OR at
   and
   de – of OR from
   When the above to prepositions merge with the definite articles they give the following contracted articles.
   Les articles contractés (contracted articles) with the preposition À are:
   À + LE = AU
   Ex. au garçon – to the boy, au restaurant – at/to the restaurant etc
   À + LA = À LA
   Ex. à la fille – to the girl, à la salle – to/at the room etc.
   À + L' = À L'
   Ex. à l'homme – to the man, à l'école – at/to the school etc.
   À + LES = AUX
   Ex. aux enfants – to the students, aux États Unis – to the USA etc.
   Examples in a sentence of les articles contractés with the preposition "À"

   a. Je donne le stylo au garçon – I give the pen to the boy.
   b. Nous allons au restaurant - We go to the restaurant.
   c. Le livre appartient à la fille – The book belongs to the girl.
   d. Jack et Jill vont à l'école – Jack & Jill go to school.
   e. Les Lenoir partent aux États Unis – The Lenoirs (surname) depart to the US.

   Les articles contractés (contracted articles) with the preposition DE:

De + LE = DU
Ex. du garçon – of the boy, du restaurant – from/of the restaurant etc
De + LA = DE LA
Ex. de la fille – of the girl, de la salle – from/of the room etc.
De + L' = D L'
Ex. de l'homme – of the man, de l'école – from/of the school etc.
De + LES = DES
Ex. des enfants – of the students, des États Unis – from/of the USA etc.

Examples in a sentence of les articles contractés with the preposition "DE"

a. C'est le livre du professeur – This is the teacher's book/ book of the teacher.
b. La famille Lavigne revient du jardin – The Lavigne family is coming back from the garden.
c. J'ai le cahier de l'homme – I have the man's book / book of the man.
d. C'est la robe de la fille – this is the girl's dress / dress of the girl.
e. Les Lenoir rentrent des États Unis – The Lenoirs (surname) return from the US.

In English we would not say, "I give the pen to the Shyam" or "I read the book of the Ram." As "to the, of the, from then" don't go with a proper noun.

Similar is the case with French, we will not use partitive articles before the proper nouns. What follows are a few examples of the same.

Ex.

i. Le professeur donne le cahier à Martha. - The teacher gives the book to Martha.
ii. Je parle à M. Tom. - I speak to Mr. Tom.

iii. C'est le stylo de Paul. - This is Mr. Paul's pen.

4. **Les articles partitifs:**

Everyone is a consumer and so everyone consumes something or the other. But the fact is that we can not consume everything at once.

An example given is that one can't drink all the water on earth, will he?

No. so, he'll drink some water. He'll buy some chips, drink some wine etc etc.

This word "some" in French is called a partitive article, rightly so, because we can just consume a part of whatever we want or need for that matter.

What follows is the formation of partitive articles according to the gender of the verb being talked about.

De + le = du
Ex.
Je bois du vin. – I drink some wine.
Ils achètent du dessert. – They buy some dessert.
De + la = de la
Ex.
J'achète de la bière. – I buy some wine.
Nous mangeons de la pizza. – we eat some pizza.
De + l' = de l'
Ex.
Jacques boit de l'eau. – Jacques drinks some water.
Passe-moi de l'huile d'olive. – Pass me some olive oil.
De + les = des
Ex.
Nous mangeons des frites. – we eat some French-fries.
Je mange des pates le dimanche. – I eat pasta on Sundays.

CHAPTER THREE
LES ADJECTIFS

After the nouns and the articles we thought that it would be interesting for you to know how to describe a noun. All the noun describing words like in English are called "les adjectifs".

The most important thing in the adjectives is that they will agree with the number and the gender of the noun that is been described i.e. if the noun that we are talking of is feminine we'll have to add an 'e' the adjective and if it is plural we'll have to add a 's'.

Exceptions to the above rules are:

The adjectives that already end with "e" will not take an extra "e" in the feminine.

The adjectives that already end with "s" will not take an extra "s" in the plural.

You shall find out more about it in the following format:

1. ENGLISH
2. MASCULINE SINGULAR
3. MASCULINE PLURAL
4. FEMININE SINGULAR
5. FEMININE PLURAL

1. Tall/big
2. grand
3. grands
4. grande

5. grandes

1. Small/short
2. petit
3. petits
4. petite
5. petites

1. Thin
2. mince
3. minces
4. mince
5. minces

1. Fat
2. gros
3. gros
4. grosse
5. grosses

1. Cheerful
2. souriant
3. souriants
4. souriante
5. souriantes

1. High
2. haut
3. hauts
4. haute
5. hautes

1. Low
2. bas
3. bas

4. basse
5. basses

1. Strong
2. fort
3. forts
4. forte
5. fortes

1. Happy
2. content
3. contents
4. contente
5. contentes

1. Sad
2. triste
3. tristes
4. triste
5. tristes

1. Naughty
2. méchant
3. méchants
4. méchante
5. méchantes

1. Thin
2. mince
3. minces
4. mince
5. minces

1. Narrow
2. étroit

3. étroits
4. étroite
5. étroites

1. Old
2. ancien
3. anciens
4. ancienne
5. anciennes

1. New
2. nouveau
3. nouveaux
4. nouvelle
5. nouvelles

1. Old (age)
2. vieux
3. vieux
4. vieille
5. vieilles

1. Young
2. jeune
3. jeunes
4. jeune
5. jeunes

1. Intelligent
2. Intelligent
3. Intelligents
4. Intelligente
5. Intelligentes

1. Stupid

2. bête
3. bêtes
4. bête
5. bêtes

1. Funny
2. amusant
3. amusants
4. amusante
5. amusantes

1. Pretty
2. joli
3. jolis
4. jolie
5. jolies

1. Beautiful
2. beau
3. belle
4. beaux
5. belles

1. Ugly
2. laid
3. laids
4. laide
5. laides

1. Nice/kind
2. gentil
3. gentils
4. gentille
5. gentilles

1. Plesant
2. sympha
3. symphas
4. sympha
5. symphas

1. Unhappy
2. mécontent
3. mécontents
4. mécontente
5. mécontentes

1. Good
2. bon
3. bons
4. bonne
5. bonnes

1. Bad
2. mauvais
3. mauvais
4. mauvaise
5. mauvaises

1. Wonderful
2. formidable
3. formidables
4. formidable
5. formidables

1. Black
2. noir
3. noirs
4. noire
5. noires

1. White
2. blanc
3. blancs
4. blanche
5. blanches

1. Grey
2. gris
3. gris
4. grise
5. grises

1. Red
2. rouge
3. rouges
4. rouge
5. rouges

1. Orange
2. orange
3. orange
4. orange
5. orange

There are a few more adjectives. What's mentioned above are used frequently.

Examples in a sentence:

1. le garçon est grand – la fille est grande.

    The boy is tall/big – the girl is tall/big.

2. Sameer est petit – sameera est petite.

    Sameer is short/small – Sameera is short/small.

3. Sam et Peirre sont méchants – Priya et Priyal sont méchantes.

   Sam and Pierre are naughty – Priya and Priyal are naughty.

4. Scooby et Shaggy sont forts – Wilma et Daffny sont fortes.

   Scooby et Shaggy are strong - Wilma et Daffny are strong.

Placement of adjectives:

Many of the adjectives are places after the noun unlike the English language where we see that the adjectives are standing after the noun.
   Ex.
   A handsome boy.
   The old lady.
   A brown book.
   A circular table.
   In French it's the other way around – many or most of the adjectives stand **after** the noun. They are as follows:
   Adjectives of nationality:
   Ex.
   C'est une fille française. – This is a French girl.
   Marc et Pascal sont les hommes canadiens. – Marc and Pascal are Canadian men.
   Adjectives of color:
   Ex.
   C'est un stylo noir. – This is a black pen.
   Ce sont les fleurs roses. – These are pink flowers.
   Adjectives of form and shapes:
   C'est une porte étroite. – This is a narrow door.
   C'est une table ronde. – This is a circular/round table.

There are a few short adjectives that are placed before the noun. They are as follows:

1. Petit – c'est un petit garçon.
2. Grand – le garçon a un grand chien.
3. Bon – c'est un bon élève.
4. Mauvais – c'est le mauvais temps.
5. Vieux – ma mère a une vieille soeur.
6. Nouveau – il y a un nouveau étudiant dans notre classe.
7. Faux – c'est un faux nouvelle.
8. Vrai – c'est un vrai frère.
9. Jeune – j'ai une jeune ami.
10. Beau / belle – c'est un beau acteur / c'est une belle actrice.
11. Gros – Rohit est un gros garçon.
12. Gentil – me grand-mère est une gentile dame.
13. Joli – c'est un joli oiseau.
14. Chaque – je vais à l'école chaque jour.
15. Dernier – l'année dernière je suis allé au Canada.
16. Tout – tout le monde sont intelligents.
17. Premier – M. Modi est notre premier minister.
18. Autre – c'est une autre fille qui a vole ma coeur.
19. Quelque – j'achète quelque bouteille de vin.
20. Plusiers – Mon frère a plusiers d'amis.

Please take a note of the following:
"DES" BECOMES "DE" WHENEVERTHERE'S AN ADJECTIVE BEFORE THE NOUN IN THE PLURAL.
Ex.
J'ai un stylo bleu but it will be j'ai __de__ gros livres.
Ce sont des filles belges but it will be ce sont __de__ belles filles.
C'est un beau garçon but it will be ce sont __de__ beaux garcons.

CHAPTER FOUR

ADJECTIVES POSSESSIFS:

These adjectives are used to show the possession of a thing.

The most important thing to remember here is that its usage depends on the gender and number of the thing in possession and not the subject.

To give an example of this we can see the Hindi word *"a book"* which is feminine and therefore even if Sharad says that it's my book, he'll say, *"yeh meri kitaab hai"* similarly taking the noun *"a brother"* which is masculine, Sonali will have to say, *"yeh mera bhai hai"* meaning, *"he's my brother."* Just by the usage of the word *"mera"* Sonali doesn't become a boy, nor does Sharad become a girl by using the word *"meri"* but those words are used to indicate that, the book is feminine and that her brother is masculine.

What follows is a Subject pronom-wise explaination of each of adjectives possessifs which will help us understand this topic better.

SUBJECT
MASCULINE
FEMININE
PLURAL OF BOTH
JE
mon
ma
mes

TU
ton
ta
tes
IL/ELLE
son
sa
ses
NOUS
notre
notre
nos
VOUS
votre
votre
vos
ILS/ELLES
leur
leur
leurs

Taking the above examples from the Hindi language, French follows the same rule. Hence, we shall see a few examples in French.

1. C'est mon stylo. – This is my pen. (doesn't matter if the person who possesses is masculine or feminine.)
2. C'est sa trousse. – This is his/her pencilbox. . (doesn't matter if the person who possesses is masculine or feminine. As the pencilbox is feminine we will use the feminine possessive adjective here.)
3. La tante de Peter, c'est sa tante. – Peter's aunt, it's his aunt.
4. C'est son crayon. – its his/her pencil.

CHAPTER FIVE

ADJECTIVES DÉMONSTRATIVES

These adjectives are used to demonstrate the relative position of a noun and they replace the definite article. They are ce, cet, cette and ces, they all mean this or these. The table that follows gives a proper picture which will be followed by relevant examples.

GENDER & NUMBER
DEMONSTRATIVE ADJECTIVES
Masculine singular
ce – *ce* garçon – this boy
Masculine singular (starting with a vowel)
cet – *cet* homme – this man
Feminine singular
cette – *cette* fille – this girl
Plural for both genders
ces – *ces* garcons/filles – these boys/girls
Ex. –

a. This boy – ce garçon
b. This man – cet homme
c. This girl – cette fille
d. These pens – ces stylos

We could use them in a sentence as follows:

1. Ce garçon est mon frère. – This boy is my brother.
2. Cet homme est mon père. – This man is my father.
3. Cetter dame est ma femme. – This lady is my wife.
4. Ces étudiants sont de classe neuvième. – These are grade 9 students.

CHAPTER SIX

VERBS

To understand any verb and how to use that verb in a sentence, we will first have to learn about the subject pronouns, with which a verb is conjugated to have a proper meaning to it.

Just like in any language we have subject pronouns like "I", "you", "he/she" etc.

The subject pronouns in the French language are as follows:

Je – I
Tu – you
il – he
Elle – she
Nous – we
Vous – you (formal or plural)
Ils – they (m)
Elles – they (f)

The conjugations of each of them with the different verbs are specific. Having said that the "il" and "elle" will always have the same conjugation. Also "ils" and "elles" will have the same conjugation.

There are 3 main categories of verbs in French – they are :
"ER" ending verbs
"IR" ending verbs and
"RE" ending verbs.
Lets see how to conjugate the above.
"ER" ending verbs

Here you will take the infinitive form of the verb – drop the "er" and then add the endings.

The endings are as follows:

Je – e
Tu – es
Il/elle – e
Nous – ons
Vous – ez
Ils/elles - ent

Ex.

<u>Parler – to speak</u>

je parle - I speak
tu parles - you speak
il/elle parle - he/she speaks
nous parlons - we speak
vous parlez - you'll speak
ils/elles parle - they speak

"IR" ending verbs

Here you will take the infinitive form of the verb – drop the "ir" and then add the endings.

The endings are as follows:

Je – is
Tu – is
Il/elle – it
Nous – issons
Vous – issez
Ils/elles - issent

Ex:

<u>Finir – to finish</u>

Je finis - I finish
tu finis - you finish
il/elle finit - he/she finishes
nous finissons - we finish
vous finissez - you'll finish
ils finissent - they finish

"RE" ending verbs.

Here you will take the infinitive form of the verb – drop the "re" and then add the endings.

The endings are as follows:

Je – s
Tu – e
Il/elle - ___(nothing)
Nous – ons
Vous – ez
Ils/elles - ent

E.g. -<u>Attendre – to wait</u>

j'attends - I wait
tu attends - you wait
il/elle attend - he/she waits
nous attendons - we wait
vous attendez - you'll wait
ils/elles attendent - they wait

There are many irregular verbs which are having the er, re, or ir ending but do not follow the above rules for conjugation. We will discuss a few of these verbs a bit later in the book.

Negative

We have to make a sentence negative, and that's the way how life works. If there is black, there has to be white. If someone is overeating someone is starving. So negative is a way to explain the opposites.

In English it is very widely used.

For example, I am fat – I am not fat. We are rich – we aren't rich. And the list goes on.

Similarly, in French we have negative and is exactly similar to the English way of formation and usage. Where we take the verb and add "ne" before it and "pas" after it.

NE + VERB + PAS

Ex.

1. Je suis gros. – je **ne** suis **pas** gros. I am fat – I am not fat.
2. Nous sommes riches. – nous **ne** sommes **pas** riches. We are rich – we aren't rich.

When the verb is beginning with a vowel the "ne" will drop its "e" and become N' in the negative as two vowels can't stand together when one is a verb.
N' + VERB (BEGINNING WITH A VOWEL) + PAS
Ex.

1. Martin écoute de la musique. – Martin **n'**écoute **pas** de musique. Martin listens to music. – Martin doesn't listen to music.
2. Vous avez cinq maisons. – vous **n'**avez **pas** cinq maisons. You have 5 houses. – You don't have 5 houses.

One of the most important rules is that the indefinite articles and the partitive articles change to "DE" in the negative with the exception if the verb used is "Être". You might think that this looked so simple in the beginning and now it's getting more and more complex. Trust me, it's the same in English but as we've been using since our birth we don't tend to notice its complexity. Take for example the sentence, "I have a pen" so the negative will be "I don't have any pen" so the "a" changed to "any" but none of us complained because that's our base language and we've been using it since childhood, so we let it slip past.

So in French un, une, des, du, de la and de l' will all change to "de" in the negative sentence.

Ex.

1. J'ai un stylo – je n'ai pas de stylo. I have a pen – I don't have any pen.

Marcella mange de l'hamburger – Marcella ne mange pas d'hamburger. Marcella eats an hamburger – Marcella doesn't eat any hamburger.

CHAPTER SEVEN

THE BIG FIVE VERBS (FIVE IMPORTANT VERBS)

I like to call these "the big five" the most important verbs because they are not only used in present tense, but also as helping verbs in the other tenses. There are also certain expressions are attached with them. So they are very important.

Besides that, they are mostly known as irregular verbs as they do not follow a pattern of conjugation, so the easiest way is to learn them by-heart.

They in present tense are as follows.

- *Être – to be*

Je suis - Ex. Je suis un garçon – I am a boy.
Tu es - Ex. Tu es un étudiant - You are a student.
Il/elle est - Ex. il est un beau / elle est belle – he is handsome/ she is beautiful.
Nous sommes - Ex. nous sommes indiens – we are Indians.
Vous êtes - Ex. vous êtes français – you(formal) are French OR you all are French.
Ils/elles sont – ils sont grands / elles sont petites – they (m) are tall / they (f) are short.

- *Avoir – to have*

J'ai - Ex. j'ai un stylo – I have a pen.
Tu as - Ex. Tu as une gomme - You have an eraser.
Il/elle a - Ex. il a des livre / elle a des livre – he has some books/ she has some books.
Nous avons - Ex. nous avons une belle robe – we have a beautiful dress.
Vous avez - Ex. vous avez une règle – you(formal) have a ruler OR you all have a ruler.
Ils/elles ont – ils ont une maison/ elles ont une maison – they(m) have a house/ they(f) have a house.

- *Aller – to go*

Je vais - Ex. je vais à l'école – I go to the school.
Tu vas - Ex. tu vas à Mumbai – you go to Mumbai.
Il/elle va - Ex. il/elle va au restaurant – he/she goes to the restaurant.
Nous allons - Ex. nous allons aux États Unis – we go to the USA.
Vous allez - Ex. Vous allez au Canada - you(formal) go to Canada OR you all go to Canada.
Ils/elles vont - Ex. ils/elles vont au cinéma/ elles vont à la banque – they(m) go to the cinema / they(f) go to the bank.

- *Venir – to come*

Je viens - Ex. je viens de l'école – I come from the school.
Tu viens - Ex. tu viens de Mumbai – you come from Mumbai.
Il/elle vient - Ex. il/elle vient du restaurant – he/she comes from the restaurant.
Nous venons - Ex. nous venons des États Unis – we come from the USA.
Vous venez - Ex. Vous venez du Japon - you(formal) come from Japan OR you all come from Japan.

Ils/elles viennent - Ex. ils/elles viennent au cinéma/ elles vont à la banque – they(m) come from the cinema / they(f) come from the bank.

- *Faire – to do / to make*

Je fais - Ex. je fais le gâteau – I make the cake.
Tu fais - Ex. Tu fais le devoir - You do the homework.
Il/elle fait - Ex. il fait la vaisselle/ elle fait la vaisselle – he does the dishes/ she does the dishes.
Nous faisons - Ex. nous faisons du bruit – we make noise.
Vous faites - Ex. vous faites l'affiche – you(formal) make the poster OR you all make the poster.
Ils/elles font – ils/elles font des etudes – they(m/f) do studies.

CHAPTER EIGHT

Pronominal verbs (reflexive verbs)

There are many verbs that we do ourselves, for example – to brush (nobody helps us brush), to bathe / shower (nobody bathes us) and many more.

In French these verbs are called pronominal verbs or the "se" verbs.

These verbs as a bit different as they are made up of two parts and both the parts have to be conjugated. It has the "se" part and the main verb.

What follows is a list of how the "se" is conjugated, and the verb is easy to conjugate as we have learnt how to conjugate them.

"se" (whoever)self
Je – me – myself
Tu – te – yourself
Il/elle – se – himself or herself
Nous – nous – ourselves
Vous – vous – yourselves
Ils / elles – se – theirselves

Lets see how these are conjugated and used in our day to day life.

Se brosser – to brush(ones teeth or hair depending on the context).

Je me brosse – I brush myself
Tu te brosses – you brush yourself

Il/elle se brosse – he/she brushes himself/herself
Nous nous brossons – we brush ourselves
Vous vous brossez – you brush yourselves
Ils/elles se brossent – they brush themselves
Se laver – to take a shower
Je me lave – I take a shower
Tu te laves – you take a shower
Il/elle se lave – he/she takes a shower
Nous nous lavons – we take a shower
Vous vous lavez – you'll take a shower
Ils/elles se lavent – they take a shower

To make the pronominal verbs negative we shall follow the same rule as how to make a sentence negative.

Ne + verb + pas

Ex.

1. Je me lave à 6h du matin – je **ne** me lave **pas** à 6h du matin.

   I shower at 6:00AM – I do not shower at 6:00AM.

2. Mes ami se promènent dans le jardin – mes amis **ne** se promènent **pas** dans le jardin.

   My friends take a walk in the garden. - My friends do not take a walk in the garden.

CHAPTER NINE
Irregular verbs

These are verbs that fit in one of the groups (ER/IR/RE) but they have certain changes when it comes to a few conjugation.

"GER" ending verbs
E.g.
Manger – to eat
Je mange
Tu manges
Il/elle mange
Nous mang**e**ons
Vous mangez
Ils/elles mangent

"Yer" ending verbs
Envoyer – to sent
J'envo**ie**
Tu envo**ies**
Il/elle envo**ie**
Nous envoyons
Vous envoyez
Ils/elles envo**ient**

Acheter – to buy
J'ach**è**te
Tu ach**è**tes
Il/elle ach**è**te
Nous achetons

Vous achetez
Ils/elles ach**è**tent
*(The verb peser – to weigh, will be conjugated similarly ex. je p**è**se...)*

Commencer – to begin / start
Je commence
Tu commences
Il/elle commence
Nous commen**ç**ons
Vous commencez
Ils/elles commencent
*(The verb placer – to place, will be conjugated similarly ex. nous pla**ç**ons...)*

Appeler – to call
J'appe**ll**e
Tu appe**ll**ee
Il/elle appe**ll**e
Nous appelons
Vous appelez
Ils/elles appe**ll**ent
(The verb jetter – to throw, will be conjugated similarly just instead of "ll" we'll use "tt" ex. je jette...)

Vouloir – to wish / want
Je veux
Tu veux
Il/elle veut
Nous voulons
Vous voulez
Ils/elles veulent

Pouvoir – to be able to / can
Je peux
Tu peux
Il/elle peut
Nous pouvons
Vous pouvez

Ils/elles peuvent

"TIR" ending verbs
Partir – to leave
Je pars
Tu pars
Il/elle part
Nous partons
Vous partez
Ils/elles partent
(The verbs sortir – to leave – je sors etc.
Sentir – to smell – tu sens etc.
Mentir – to lie, will be conjugated similarly)

Boire – to drink
Je bois
Tu bois
Il/elle boit
Nous buvons
Vous buvez
Ils/elles boivent

"RIRE" ending verbs
Décrier – to describe
Je decries
Tu decries
Il/elle décrit
Nous décrivons
Vous déceivez
Ils/elles décrivent

All verbs ending with "rire" like écrire, sourire etc will be conjugated similarly

There are many more, but to list all of them will be a bit exhaustive.

CHAPTER TEN

LES EXPRESSIONS NEGATIFS

This is not a concept in English as there are no expressions as such in English for nefaives. Therefore I would like to simplify this topics name to "absolute negation" which we use in English very often.

E.g.- I have a pen. – I don't have any pen.

We went somewhere. – We didn't go anywhere. Etc.

In French there is a list of these negations, they are as follows:

+ve – Quelque chose – something – je bois quelque chose – I drink something.

-ve – ne + verb + rien – nothing - je ne bois rien – I don't drink anything.

+ve – Quelqu'un – someone – je vois quelqu'un – I see someone.

-ve – ne + verb + personne – je ne vois personne – I see nobody / I see no one.

+ve – quelqu'un + verb – quelqu'un vient – someone comes/ came.

-ve – personne + ne + verb – personne ne vient.

+ve – quelque part – somewhere – nous allons quelque part – we go somewhere.

-ve – ne + verb + nulle part – nowhere – nous n'allons nulle part – we go nowhere.

+ve – Toujours – always – je mange toujours mes lentils – I always eat my vegetables.

-ve – ne + verb + jamais – never – je ne mange jamais mes lentils – I never eat my vegetables.

+ve – encore – still – mon frère est encore à l'école – my brother is still at school.

-ve – ne + verb + plus – no more – mon frère n'est plus à l'école – my brother is no more in school.

+ve – déjà – already – elle est déjà là – she's already there.

-ve – ne + verb + pas encore – elle n'est pas encore là – she's not yet there.

+ve (article défini) le..... et la... etc – this and that – les enfants aiment le chocolat et les bonbons. – the children like the chocolate and the sweets.

-ve – ne + verb + ni le .... ni la... etc – neither this nor that – les enfants n'aiment ni le chocolat ni les bonbons. – The children like neither the chocolate nor the sweets.

+ve (article indéfini) in.... et une... etc – this and that – les enfants aiment un chocolat et des bonbons. – the children like chocolate and sweets.

-ve – ne + verb + ni .... ni... etc – neither this nor that – les enfants n'aiment ni chocolat ni bonbons. – The children like neither chocolate nor sweets.

CHAPTER ELEVEN

LE COMPARATIF ET SUPERLATIF

Comparison is the way how everyone in the world sees everyone around themselves. People compare their weight, size, intelligence and the list is never ending. What they are really comparing are two nouns using an adjective. To cite an example, we can say. Paul is taller than Marc. So Paul and Marc are the two nouns and tall is the adjective.

We have a very similar way of comparing things, nouns, people etc in French too. As explained below we have three ways to compare i.e. positive, negative and equal.

- <u>Positive = more than</u>

  Plus + adjective + que = more adjective than
  Ex.

1. Il est plus grand que moi = he is taller (more tall) than me.
2. Shah est plus beau que Rukh. = Shah is more handsome than Rukh.

- <u>Negative = less than</u>

  Moins + adjective + que = less adjective than

Ex.

1. Araam est moins intelligent que Ram. = Araam is less intelligent than Ram.
2. Usain court moins vite que Bolt. = Usain runs slower (less fast) than Bolt.

- **Equal = equally as**

    Aussi + adjective + que = as adjective as
    Ex.

1. Prisha est aussi belle que Priya. = Prisha is as beautiful as Priya.
2. Nous sommes aussi minces que vous. = we are as thin as you.

Le Superlatif

We see around that everyone wants to be the best. Someone wants to be the most intelligent and someone wants to be the most beautiful. Everyone wants to be the best is their field.

In French we also use superlative degree to prove a point of being the best or something else to be the worst. So we shall see both ways in the explanation given below, how to say the same.

Positive = the best
Le/la/les plus + adjective = the best + adjective
Ex.

a. Amitabh est *le plus grand* acteur. = Amitabh is the tallest actor.
b. Cette trousse est *la plus grande* trousse de tout le monde. = this pencilbox is the biggest the anyone has.

c. Nous sommes **_les plus intelligents_** dans notre école. = we are the most intelligent in the whole school.

<u>Negative = the worst</u>
Le/la/les + moins = the worst/least + adjective
Ex.

a. Putana est **_la moins belle_**. = Putana is the least beautiful (the ugliest)
b. Ma soeur is **_la plus sympathique_** du monde. = My sister is the least kind (sselfish) in the whole world.

Les étudiants de deuxième classe sont **_les moins méchants_**. = the students of grade two are the least naughty.

CHAPTER TWELVE

LES PRONOMS OBJETS

This is used to replace the nouns and make shorter sentences.

Pronom toniques:

These pronouns replace the subject pronouns. They mainly are used to highlight the subject pronoun and are also used after a preposition.

The replaced subject pronoun becomes:
Je – moi
Tu – toi
Il – lui
Elle – elle
Nous – nous
Vous – vous
Ils – leur
Elles – elles

Some examples of this pronom are:

a. Moi, je m'appelle Rick. – Me, my name is Rick.
b. Lui, il est français. – He, he is French.
c. Elles, elles sont étudiantes. – They, they are students.
d. Mox va à l'école avec moi. - Mox goes to school with me.

Pronoms objet directs (direct objects - COD):

- These pronouns replace the nouns that stand directly after the verb.
- It has definite article or adjective demonstrative /possessives before it.
- After replacing the noun, it will become "le, la, l' or les" according to the gender and the number of the replaced noun.
- The subject pronouns will be replaced as follows:

je - me
Tu - te
il/Elle - le/la
Nous - nous
Vous - vous
ils/Elles - les
Ex –

a. Christine prend **le stylo**.

   Christine *le* prend.
   b. Penso donne **son crayon**.
   Penso *le* donne.

Pronoms objet indirects (indirect objects - COI):

- These pronouns replace the nouns that stand after a preposition (à) after the verb.

- These will mostly be subject pronouns or people.
- The subject pronouns will be replaced as follows:

je - me
Tu - te
il/Elle - lui
Nous - nous
Vous - vous
ils/Elles – leur
Ex –

a. Christine ne téléphone pas **à Marc**.

   Christine ne **lui** telephone pas.

b. Je donne les livres **aux étudiants**.

   Je **leur** donne les livres.

Pronom En:

This pronoun will replace *a noun* which is preceded by an article partitif (du, de la, des, de l') or an indefinite article (un, une, des).

It will also replace *a place* which is preceded by an article contracté (du, de la, des, de l').

Ex.

a. Je mange *__des frites__*. – j'*__en__* mange.
b. Priya vient *__deGoa__*. – Priya *__en__* vient.

Pronom Y:

This pronoun will replace <u>a noun</u> which is preceded by the preposition "à"

It will also replace <u>*a place*</u> which is preceded by an article contracté (au, à la, aux, à l') or the prepositions like à, chez, en, dans and sur
Ex.

a. Je pense <u>*à mes vacances d'été*</u>. – J'*y* pense.
b. Margarite va <u>*auCanada*</u>. – Margarite *y* va.

The replaced pronoun will stand in the following places:

I. *In the tenses that have only one word conjugation e.g.- present tense, future simple etc.*

   It will stand between the subject pronoun and the verb.
   Ex.

a. j'achète <u>le stylo</u>. – I buy the pen.

   Je l'achete – I buy that.

b. Sanjana ne donnera pas <u>les robes</u>. – Sanjana will not give the dresses.

   Sanjana ne **les** donnera pas – Sanjana will gives those.

c. J'aime <u>mes amis</u>. – I like my friends.

Je **les** aime- I like them.

II. *In the tenses that uses past participle e.g. passé compose, futur antérieur etc it will stand between the subject and the helping verb.*

   Ex.

a. Nusrat a lu <u>le livre</u>. – Nusrat read the book.

   Nusrat l'a lu. – Nusrat read that.

b. Roopali aura vu <u>la télévision</u>. – Roopali will watch T.V.

   Roopali l'aura vu. – Roopali will watch that.

III. *In the tenses that need 2 verbs to form a proper conjugation e.g. futur proche etc. it will stand between the two verbs i.e. the helping verb and the main verb.*

   Ex.

a. Mark va manger des frites.

   Mark va <u>**en**</u> manger.

b. Nous devons apprendre le français.

   nous devons <u>L</u>'apprendre.

IV. *In an impératif sentence - it will stand after the verb*
   Ex.

a. Mange des frites!

   Mange - <u>**en !**</u>

b. Allons à Paris!

Allons-*y!*

V. *In an impératif negatif - it will stand between the NE & the VERB*
Ex.

a. Ne Mange pas des frites!

N'*en* mange pas!

b. Ne va pas dans ce restaurant!

N'*y* va pas!

Please note:

when there are more than one pronoun to be used in a sentence - their position will be as following.

SUBJECT + (NE -in a negative sentence) = SUBJECT PRONOUNS + COD + COI +Y + EN+ VERB + PAS

Ex.
Je donne le stylo à Marc. - I give the pen to Marc.
Je lelui donne. - I give him that.

Les pronoms possessifs (possessive pronouns)

Just like the adjective pronouns these indicate possession of a noun by the subject. The only difference here is that the noun is not used, just the pronoun is used instead of it and because this pronoun shows possession it is called possessive pronoun. We often use in English one word answers for questions pertaining possession.

e.g. –

Q. - Who's book is this?

Ans. – Mine, his/hers etc.

Here too the pronouns will follow the gender and number of the possession (thing) and not the possessor(person who has/possesses the thing). The following table will give you a crystal clear understanding of the same.

SUBJECT
MASCULINE SINGULAR
MASCULINE PLURAL
FEMINIE SINGULAR
FEMININE PLURAL
JE
le mien
les miens
la mienne
les miennes
TU
le tien
les tiens
la tienne
les tiennes
IL/ELLE
le sien
les sien
la sienne
les siennes
NOUS
le nôtre
les nôtres
la nôtre
les nôtres

VOUS
le vôtre
les vôtres
la vôtre
les vôtres
ILS/ELLES
le leur
les leurs
la leur
les leurs

A few examples can be cited for better understand are as follows:

a. Mon stylo est bleu, de quelle couleur est le tien? - My pen is blue, what color is yours?
b. C'est ma maison, où est la sienna? - This is my house, where is his/hers (according to the subject)?
c. Son stylo ne marche pas, emprunte le tien. - His pen isn't working borrow yours.

Les pronoms démonstratives

Identical to adjectives demonstratives they also mean "this / that / these" the only difference is that we shall not use the noun as this pronoun will replace it.

GENDER & NUMBER DEMONSTRATIVE PRONOUNS
Masculine singular *celui*
Masculine Plural *ceux*
Feminine singular *celle*
Feminine Plural *celles*

We should also learn that "ci" is short for "voici" which means "here" and "là" is short for "voilà" which means "there" and when these words are used with a demonstrative pronoun it will mean "this one here" or "that one there". Hence, they are called "adjectives démonstratives composes"

GENDER & NUMBER Form compose with "ci" Form compose with "là"

Masculine singular *celui-ci* – this one here *celui-là* – that one there

Masculine Plural c*eux-ci* – these here *ceux- là* - those there

Feminine singular *celle-ci* - this one here *celle- là* - this one there

Feminine Plural *celles-ci* – these here *celles- là* – those there

A few examples that will illustrate the above are:

- Regarde cette robe. (look at this dress)
- Laquelle? Celle-ci en soie? (which one? Silk one?)
- Non, celle-là en coton (no, the cotton one)

- Qui est le voleur? Celui-ci ou celui-là? (who is the thief, this one here or that one there?)

There are also neutral pronouns: Neutral demonstrative pronoms are used when the subject is not specified. Generally, the imperative sentences don't specify the noun so its difficult to find out its gender. Therefore we use gender-neutral demonstrative pronouns. They are *<u>ceci, cela</u>* and *<u>ce</u>*.

E.g. - Ne bois pas *<u>ceci/cela</u>* (don't drink <u>*that*</u>)

<u>Cela</u> n'est pas vrai. (<u>*that*</u> isn't true)

Pronoms relatifs

They are generally used to join 2 sentences. When the two sentences are joined they shall replacing the object in the second sentence.

They are:

- QUI – that, which, who – it should always have a verb after it.

    Ex. Je veux un stylo. *Il* est noir.
    Je veux un stylo *qui* est noir.

- QUE – that, which

    Ex. Le diwali est une fête spécial. Les enfants *L'*aiment beaucoup.
    Le diwali est une fête spécial *que* les enfants aiment beaucoup.

- OÙ – where

    Ex. c'est une maison. Je suis né dans ***cette maison***.
    c'est une maison *où* je suis né

- DONT – whose/ of who

    Ex. Salman est un étudiant. Je suis fier ***de salman***.
    Salman est un étudiant dont je suis fier.

Pronom relative composé

This is formed by adding together a preposition, a definite article and interrogative adjective.

When a definit article and an interrogative adjective adds up the English translation of that word is "which".

e.g –

- le+quel = lequel = which (masculine/singular).

- la + quelle = laquelle = which (feminine/singular)

- les + quels = lesquels = which (masculine/ plural)

- les + quelles = lesquelles = which (feminne/ plural)

and when you add preposition before it, it becomes – preposition + which.
e.g. –
dans + lequel = dans lequel – C'est un sac ***dans lequel*** je met mes livres. – This is a bag ***in which*** I keep my books.
Sur + laquelle = surlaquelle – C'est la table ***sur laquelle*** j'étudie. – This is a table ***on which*** I study.
When these pronouns are used with the preposition "à" and "de" they will change a bit and presume the beginning of "the contracted articles"
With préposition **à**
à + Lequel = auquel
à + laquelle = à laquelle
à + lesquels = auxquels
à + lesquelles = auxquelles
With préposition **de**
de + Lequel = duquel
de+ laquelle = de laquelle
de + lesquels = desquels
de + lesquelles = desquelles
The following examples can help us understand the above:

- C'est le livre ***duquel*** je parle – this is the book ***of what/which*** I'm speaking.

- La route _à laquelle_ ils sont passé est glissante. – the route that they took is slippery.

CHAPTER THIRTEEN
TENSES - PASSÉ COMPOSÉ

Tenses are what give the language some sense of time. Like in English or any other language. In French too we have many tenses. In this book we will be discussing the tenses which are actually used at school level as this is a handbook for the school students.

Out of the many tenses, let's get started with the one that is very important and helpful in many other tenses – as we have already learnt how to conjugate and use the verbs in present tense.

Passé composé (past tense)

This tense is used like how we use past tense in the English language. It is very easy to use in our day to day life to describe a complete action in the past.

To conjugate any verb in this tense we follow the following steps:
Take the present conjugation of « être or avoir » and add the Past participle of the main verb.

The following are the ways to make past participle of the main verb:

- Verbs ending with « er » - é - j'ai parlé – I spoke.
- Verbs ending with « ir » - i - Tu as fini - I finished.
- Verbs ending with « re » - u - Mark est venu – Mark came.

Ex.

a. J'ai mangé de la pizza. – I ate some pizza.
b. Donald Tramp a bu trop de vin. - Donald Tramp drank a lot of wine.
c. Vous avez joué au cricket pendant les vacances. – You'll played cricket during the holidays.
d. Elles ont étudié bien pour les examen. – They studied well for the exams.

There is a specific list of verbs that use "être" as an auxiliary/helping verb and it is as follows:

- Devenir – to become – *(être) devenu(e)(s)*
- Revenir – to come back – *(être) revenu(e)(s)*
- Monter – to go up – *(être) monté(e)(s)*
- Rester – to stay – *(être) resté(e)(s)*
- Sortir – to exit – *(être) sorti(e)(s)*
- Venir – to come – *(être) venu(e)(s)*
- Aller – to go – *(être) allé(e)(s)*
- Naître – to be born – *(être) né(e)(s)*
- Descendre – to descend – *(être) descendu(e)(s)*
- Entrer – to enter – *(être) entré(e)(s)*
- Retourner – to return – *(être) retourné(e)(s)*
- Tomber – to fall – *(être) tombé(e)(s)*
- Rentrer – to re-enter – *(être) rentré(e)(s)*
- Arriver – to arrive – *(être) arrivé(e)(s)*
- Mourir – to die – *(être) mort(e)(s)*
- Partir – to leave – *(être) parti(e)(s)*

*The above are commonly remembered using the acronym **DR and MRS VANDERTRAMP**.*

In addition to the above list, there the verb "passer – to pass" which takes both *"être and avoir"* as auxiliary verb, depending on the context. If the context is to pass a holiday somewhere – it will take avoir and if its used in the context of passing through a place, it will take *être*. So in short when the verb "passer" shows motion it will take *"être"* and if it isn't showing movement / motion it'll take avoir.

To cite an example we can see below:

Être - je suis passé(e) par l'école quand je suis venu(e) ici. – I passed by the school when I came here.

Avoir – j'ai passé le sel à ma mere. – I passed the salt to my mother.

You may be wondering why is there an "E" and "S" in brackets in the list of *être*???

Now here's where things get interesting. As per the rules of passé compose we have to add and "E" if the subject is feminine, a "S" if the subject is plural and "E" and "S" if the subject is feminine and plural to the past participle of the main verb.

Ex.

a. Christine est parti*e* en France. – Christine left for France.
b. Nous sommes allé*s* au restaurant hier soir. – we went to the restaurant last evening.
c. Karishma et Kareena sont devenu*es* les vedettes. - Karishma and Kareena became movie stars.

The following picture will give a better visual understanding of the *être using verbs*.

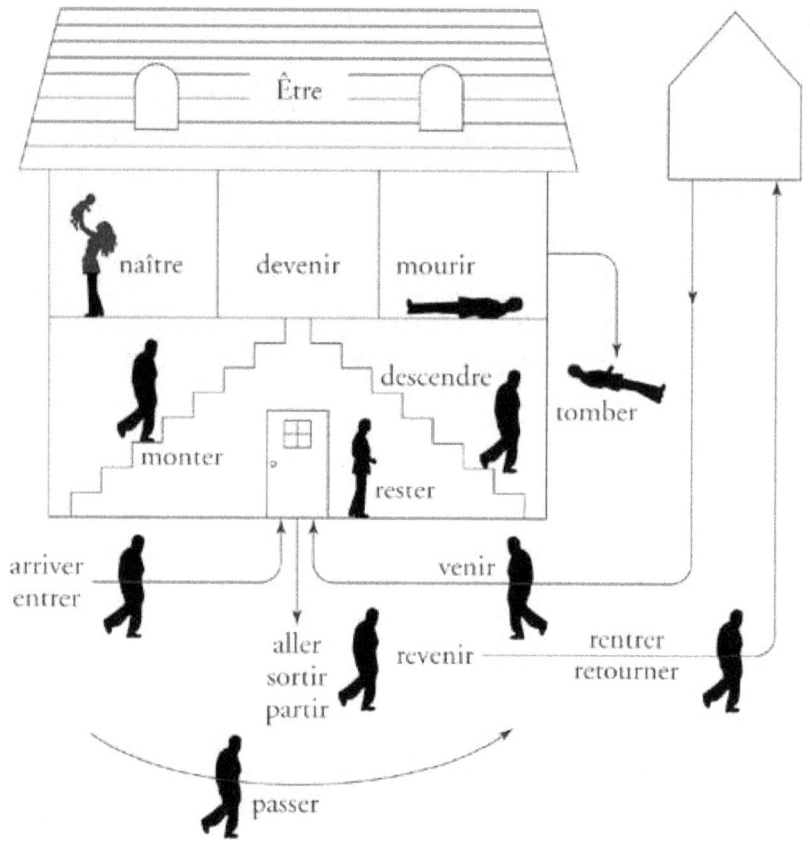

the house of être

All the pronominal verbs will also be taking *être* as an auxiliary verb. The following are a few examples of the same:

a. Je me **suis** levé(e) très tard hier. – yesterday I woke up very late.
b. Tu t'**es** brossé(e) les dents? – did you brush the teeth?
c. Elle s'**est** habillée pour aller à l'école. – she got dressed for going to school.

Ils se **sont** promenés dans le jardin. – they took a walk in the garden.

CHAPTER FOURTEEN

Tenses - Futur proche et passé récent

Futur means future and proche means near. So this tense will be translated as near future.

It doesn't have any definite rule as to how long in a time period it lasts but we can take a guess by understanding the context.

To conjugate any verb in this tense we shall do the following:

Take the present conjugation of the verb <u>"aller"</u> according to the subject used.

And add the **<u>infinitive (non-conjugated) form of the main verb</u>**.
Ex.

1. Je *vais manger* du gâteau. - I'm going to eat cake.
2. Nous *allons apprendre* le futur dans 5 minutes. - We'll be learning futur tense in 5 minutes.
3. Ma mère *va venir* à l'école demain. - My mother will come to the school tomorrow.
4. ils *vont jouer* au cricket dans quelques instants. - They're goint to play cricket in some time.

Passé Récent

Passé means past and récent means recent. So this tense is used to indicate some action that has just taken place a few moments ago or a day back.

To conjugate any verb in this tense we shall do the following:

Take the present conjugation of the verb "venir" according to the subject pronoun

+

De

+

Main verb in the infinitive form.

Ex.

English – I just ate the mango.

French – je ***viens de manger*** la mangue.

English – They just came back from Canada.

French – ils ***viennent de revenir*** du Canada.

CHAPTER FIFTEEN

Tenses - Futur Simple

This tense is used to indicate any action happening in the future, just like in the English language. This tense is very easy to conjugate and even to use.

We shall conjugate it in the following way:

For "ER" and "IR" verbs, take the infinitive form of the main verb and add the endings to it.

The endings are as follows:

Endings :

Je – ai
 Tu – as
 Il/elle – a
 Nous – ons
 Vous – ez
 Ils/elles – ont
 Following are a few verbs conjugated in this tense.
 Ex.
 Parler - to speak
 Je – parlerai – i will speak.
 Tu – Parleras – you will speak.
 Il/elle – Parlera – he/she will speak.

Nous – Parlerons – we will speak.
Vous – Parlerez – you'll will speak.
Ils/elles – Parleront – they will speak.

Finir – to finish
Je finirai – i will finish.
Tu finiras – you will finish.
Il/elle finira – he/she will finish.
Nous finirons – we will finish.
Vous finirez – you'll will finish.
Ils/elles finiront – they will finish.

For "RE" verbs, take the infinitive form of the main verb, subtract the ending "E" and add .The endings to it the endings remain the same here.

Ex.

Prendre - to take
Je – Prendrai – i will take.
Tu – Prendras – you will take.
Il/elle – Prendra – he/she will take.
Nous – Prendrons – we will take.
Vous – Prendrez – you'll will take.
Ils/elles – Prendront – they will take.

*There are a few irregular verbs that don't follow the above pattern. Which means that they slightly change the stem before adding the endings to them. A few of the regularly used verbs are as follows.

- aller → **ir** → j'**irai** - I will go
- avoir → **aur** → j'**aurai** - I will have
- être → **ser** → je **serai** - I will be
- faire → **fer** → je **ferai** - I will do
- pouvoir → **pourr** → je **pourrai** - I will be able to
- devoir → **devr** → je **devrai** - I will have to
- savoir → **saur** → je **saurai** - I will know
- venir → **viendr** → je **viendrai** - I will come
- voir → **verr** → je **verrai** - I will see

vouloir → **voudr** → je **voudrai** - I will like/want

CHAPTER SIXTEEN

Tenses - Imparfait

This tense is used for informing us that the verb is:

I. Continuously happening in the past, for example I used to be small.
II. It is also used to show an incomplete action in the past, for example when I entered the room you were washing the dishes.

To conjugate any verb in this tense we will
Take the present NOUS conjugation of the main verb
Subtract the "ONS"
Add the endings
Je - ais
Tu - ais
Il/elle - ait
Nous - ions
Vous - iez
Ils/elles - aient
Following are the exceptions to the above rule:

- être - ét + endings
- Falloir – il fallait
- Pleuvoir – il pleuvait
- Neiger – il neigait

Ex.

- I was small - j'étais petit.
- Il fallait aller à l'école. It used to be necessary to go to school.
- Hier soir, il pleuvait beaucuop.
- Hiver dernière, il neigait pour cinq jour.

Examples for regular imparfait:
A. *Continuously happening in the past*:

1. In grade ten we used to write long essays.

   Dans la dixième classe nous écrivions de longues essais.
   B. *It is used to show an incomplete action in the past*:

2. When I entered the room you were washing the dishes

   Quand je suis entré la salle tu lavais les vaisselles.

CHAPTER SEVENTEEN

Tenses - Plus que parfait (PQP)

This tense is used to indicate that an action had been taken place before another action in the past. To put it in simple words, this is "past of the past tense"

To conjugate any verb in this tense we shall do the following:

Take the imparfait conjugation of the verb "être or avoir" according to the subject used.

And add the past participle of the main verb.

*the rules on which verb takes être and which takes avoir and all the other details regarding the verbs that take être and how its past participle changes accordingly remains the same as in "passé compose".

Ex.

1. I was born in the USA, last year we came to India.

J'*étais né* aux États-Unis, nous sommes venus en Inde l'année dernière.
2. The students had a party after their exams were over.
Après leurs examens *avaient fini*, Les étudiants ont fêté.

CHAPTER EIGHTEEN
TENSES - FUTUR ANTÈRIEUR

Antèrieur means *"interior"*. So futur antèrieur means the futur tense within another future tense.

In simple terms, if there are two verbs/actions happening in the future. The first one will be conjugated in futur antèrieur.

To conjugate any verb in this tense we shall do the following:
Take the futur simple conjugation of the verb "être or avoir" according to the subject used.
And add the past participle of the main verb.
***the verbs that take "être or avoir" remain the same as in passé composé.*

Ex.

Rohit <u>sera allé</u> en France ensuite il deviendra médecin. - Rohit will go to France and then become a doctor.

je me marrierai quand j'<u>aurai fini</u> mes études. - I'll get married when i finish my education.

Désque nous aurons fini nos examens, nous irons à Agra. - so soon as our exams will get over we'll go to Agra.

**the rules on which verb takes être and which takes avoir and all the other details regarding the verbs that take être and how its past participle changes accordingly remains the same as in "passé compose".*

CHAPTER NINETEEN

Nominalisation (Noun forms)

Noun forms are made from the verbs or adjectives just like in any language. Theres no specific rule to make a verb into a noun form. Ex. Verbe : lire → la lecture Adjectif : frais → la fraîcheur. It can be done by adding a suffix at the root of the verb.

Noun forms are made from the verbs or adjectives just like in any language. Theres no specific rule to make a verb into a noun form.

Ex.

Verbe : lire → la lecture

Adjectif : frais → la fraîcheur

It can be done by adding a suffix at the root of the verb.
SUFFIX VERB NOM

-tion, ution, punir, déduire, punition, déduction

Ition, ation traduire, graduer traduction, graduation

-sion - exploser, éroder, éclore - explosion, érosion, éclosion

-ence, ance - exister, assister - existence, assistance

-ment - raisonner render - raisonnement, rendement

-age - tourner, abattre, passer - tournage, abattage, passage

-ure - souder, gager, brûler - soudure, gageure, brûlure

-ée - lever, monter, tourner, dicter - levée, montée, tournée, dictée

-ie - incendier, envier, agoniser - incendie, envie, agonie

-te, té - perdre, vendre, égaler - perte, vente, égalité
-at - assassiner, plagier - assassinat, plagiat
-ise - prendre, mépriser, maîtriser - prise, méprise, maîtrise
-ade - tirer, rouler - tirade, roulade
-xion - Connecter, fléchir, réfléchir - Connexion, flexion, réflexion
-erie - rêver, flâner, tromper - rêverie, flânerie, tromperie,
-sson - cuire, boire - cuisson, boisson

We can also do it by simple removing the endings:
VERB NOM
Débuter - le début
Ajouter - l'ajoute
Sauter - le saut
Chanter - le chant
Voler - le vol
Arrêter - l'arrêt
Finir - la fin
Appâter - l'appât

The noun form can be also be made by using the infinitive verb as it is:
VERB NOM
Rire - le rire
Sourire - le sourire
Souper - le souper
dîner - le dîner

Noun forms can be made by adding to the suffix of the adjectives.
SUFFIX VERB NOM
Le démocrate, diplomate - la démocratie, la diplomatie, aristocrate - l'aristocratie
ise - roublard, traîtr - la roublardise, la traîtrise
té - libre, égal, fraternel, sain, loyal, beau - la liberté, l'égalité, la fraternité, la santé,
la loyauté, la beauté

tude - seul, apte, exact, ample, las - la solitude, l'aptitude, l'exactitude, l'amplitude, la lassitude

ance - tolérant, suffisant - la tolérance, la suffisance

ence - différent, innocent, absent - la différence, l'innocence, l'absence

esse - hardi, paresseux, bas, vieux, sage - la hardiesse, la paresse, la bassesse, la vieillesse, la sagesse

erie - étourdi, pedant - l'étourderie, la pédanterie

eur - grand, lent, lourd, large, blanc - la grandeur, la lenteur, la lourdeur, la largeur, la blancheur

isme - réel, classique - réalisme, classicisme,

iste - naturel, national - naturaliste, nationaliste

CHAPTER TWENTY

SUBJONTIF

Let's begin by saying that this is not a tense. Due to having verbs and conjugation people get it messed up with the tenses and think that this too is a tense.

There is no exact English for subjontif, so you will have to understand it as it is. To make it easier for understanding I'll put it in points.

1. There are two subject pronouns (je, tu, il/elle etc.) used in the same sentence.
2. These two subject pronouns (je, tu, il/elle etc.) have to be different.
3. The sentence has to have the word "QUE" before the second subject pronoun.
4. The first subject pronoun must be urging the second subject pronoun to do an activity (verb) which will be conjugated in "subjontif".
5. Conjugation of subjontif is not following any particular pattern. But let's make it easier to comprehend it.

a. *For je, tu, il/elle and ils/elles:*

- Take the ils/elles conjugation of the verb in present tense
- Subtract the ending "ENT"
- And add the following endings:

Je – e
Tu – es
Il/elle – e
Ils/elles – ent

b. **For nous and vous:**

Their conjugation will remain the **_same as their imparfait_** conjugations.
Ex.
Parler
Que je parle
Que tu parles
Qu'il/elle parle
Que nous parlions
Que vous parliez
Qu'ils/elles parlent
Finir
Que je finisse
Que tu finisses
Qu'il/elle finisse
Que nous finissions
Que vous finissiez
Qu'ils/elles finissent
Boire
Que je boive
Que tu boives
Qu'il/elle boive
Que nous buvions
Que vous buviez
Qu'ils/elles boivent

As you might have already noticed in the tenses that when it comes to conjugation, there are many exceptions. Subjontif is not and exception to this rule and hence it also has a few irregular conjugations.

They are as follows:
Être – Que je sois
Avoir – Que j'aie
Savoir – Que je sache
Pouvoir – Que je puisse
Vouloir – Que je veuille
Faire – Que je fasse
Aller – Que j'aille
Falloir – Qu'il faille

Let's take a few examples and see how the above mentioned points are applied to get a sentence in subjontif:

English - I wish that you study for your exams.

French - Je veux que tu étudies pour tes examens.

In the above sentence we can observe the above 5 points broken down for better understanding:

1. The two subject pronouns – je and tu
2. Both of them are different i.e je and tu
3. There is "que" before the second subject pronoun i.e 'tu'
4. The first subject pronoun (je) is urging (in terms of wishing) the second subject pronoun(tu) to study.
5. Conjugation of étudier

    Taking ils/elles present tense form which is *étudient*
    Subtracting "ent" – remaining stem "étudi"
    Adding tu ending (es) to the remaining stem
    = Étudies

English – My father insists that we be on time for the concert.

French - Mon père insiste que nous soyons à l'heure pour le concert.

In the above sentence we can again observe the above 5 points broken down for better understanding:

1. The two subject pronouns – mon père and nous
2. Both of them are different i.e mon père and nous

3. There is "que" before the second subject pronoun i.e 'nous'
4. The first subject pronoun (mon père) is urging (in terms of insisting) the second subject pronoun(nous) to be on time.
5. Conjugation of être

   Because it is irregular we have the following conjugations for 'être'
   Que je sois
   Que tu sois
   Qu'il/elle soit
   Que nous soyons
   Que vous soyez
   Qu'ils/elles soient
   Hence nous conjugation will be "soyons"

CHAPTER TWENTY-ONE

Discour Rapporté

Many times you may not hear what's being said to you and so someone else has to repeat the same for you.

Sometimes you may forget what was been told and so someone reminds you about it.

In French there are many different ways to use direct / indirect speech.

If a question is been converted to indirect speech, it will lose (will not have) the question mark(?).

Lets see the following examples as if professor Mr. Charou is speaking to Suhani (direct) and because Suhabi isn't paying attention Riya, her friend is relaying it for her (indirect).

Declarative sentence:

Direct: <<**Il pleut** >>(its raining)

Indirect: Il dit **qu'il pleut**. (he's saying that its raining)

Impérative sentence:

Direct: <<**Viens** ici>> (come here.)

Indirect: **Il te demande de venir** ici.(He is asking you to come here)

Direct: <<**ne va pas** à la plage>> (don't go to the beach)

Indirect: **Il te demande de ne pas aller** à la plage. (he's asking you not to go to the beach)

Interrogative sentence:

Direct: <<**manges - tu** des frites?>> (are you eating fries?)

Indirect: **Il te demande si tu manges** des frites. (he's asking if you are eating fries)

Direct: <<**Qu'est ce que** tu bois?>> (what are you drinking)

Indirect: **Il te demande ce que** tu bois (he's asking what are you drinking)

Direct: <<**qui** va en France?>> (who's going to France)

Indirect: **Il te demande qui va** en France. (he's asking, who is going to France)

Direct: <<**Qu'est ce qui** t'arrive?>> (what happened to you)

Indirect: **Il te demande ce qui** t'arrive (he's asking whats happened to you)

Direct: <<**qui** invites-tu ce soir?>> (whom are you inviting this evening)

Indirect: **Il te demande qui** tu invites ce soir. (he's asking whom are you calling this evening)

Direct: <<**Comment vas-tu** à l'école?>> (how are you going to school)

Indirect: **Il te demande comment tu vas** à l'école. (he's asking how are you going to school)

Direct: <<**Quand** viens-tu chez moi?>> (when are you visiting me)

Indirect: **Il te demande quand tu** viens chez lui. (he's asking when are you visiting him)

CHAPTER TWENTY-TWO
Present participle and Grondif

There are many uses to this but at school level French we will just use it to show two verbs happening at the same time and it can be translated as 'while' or 'upon'.
Ex.
English – While being sick, I don't go to school.
French – Étant malade, je ne vais pas à l'école.
English – Upon watching a film on poverty, Marc understood the value of money.
French – Voyant un film de pauvreté , Marc a compris la valeur de l'argent.
Conjugation:
The best part of it is that present participle doesn't have a whole list of conjugations with various subject pronouns. It's like you go shopping and by a dress which is "one size fits all." Similarly present participle has only one conjugation for all the subject pronouns.
To form that we shall take the present nous conjugation of the verb
Subtrace the "ONS"
And and "ANT"
Ex. parler – parlons – parlant
Voir – voyons – voyant
The exceptions to this are as follows:

Être – étant
Avoir – ayant
Savoir – sachant

Gérondif

This is an extention of present participle – by adding "EN" before the present participle.

Ex. en ayant, en discutant etc.

It is used as an explanation of the cause and effect.

Ex.

French – Samir est tombé **_en voyant_** un serpant.

English – Samir fell when he saw the snake. / Seeing the snake, Samir fell.

French – Karl a eu de bonne notes **_en travaillant_** dur.

English – Karl got good marks by working hard.

CHAPTER TWENTY-THREE
CONDITIONNEL (PRÉSENT ET PASS)

Conditionnel isn't a tense but is used in the French language in the following ways:
Politeness:
This is used for asking for something from someone and sounds more polite.
Ex.

1. Je veux un verre d'eau – I want a glass of water. (not polite)

   Je voudrais un verre d'eau. – I would like to have a glass of water. (polite)

2. Vous pouvez m'aider = Can you help me ? (just neutral)

   Vous pourriez m'aider = Could you help ? (more polite)
   Hypothetical event
   With si (if) and another verb conjugated in imparfait, i.e. *si+imparfait+conditionnel*
   Ex.

1. Si j'étais rich, je ferais un tour du monde. – if I'd be rich, I'd do a world tour.

2. J'achèterais une voiture si je gagnais au lotto. - I'd but a car, if I'd win the lotto.

To conjugate any verb in conditionnel we shall;
Take the infinitive of the main verb
+ (add)
Endings
Endings are;
Je - ais
Tu - ais
Il/elle - ait
Nous - ions
Vous - iez
Ils/elles - aient
Ex.
Parler
Je parlerais
Tu parlerais
Il/elle parlerait
Nous parlerions
Vous parleriez
Ils/elles parleraient

The irregular verbs will follow the same stem of the futur simple and add endings:
Ex.
Avoir
J'aurais
Tu aurais
Il/elle aurait
Nous aurions
Vous auriez
Ils/elles auraient

Conditionnel passé

This is similar to the conditionnel just that this is in the past.
Hypothetical event changes to accommodate past tense here.
So with si (if) instead of imparfait we shall use plus que parfait.
i.e. si + plus que parfait + conditionnel passé = SI + PQP + CP
To conjugate a verb in conditionnel passé we shall;
Take the conditionnel form of Être or avoir
+ (add)
The past participle of the main verb
<u>Please note that the conjugation rules remain the same as in passé composé</u>

Ex.
Si tu étais né en France, tu serais été français.

Nous aurions mangé des frites si les pommes de terre n'avaient pas été chères.

Note To The Reader

This is my attempt at making French with is a subject that makes school life look difficult, easy. I'm sure that the students will love the way I have made the concepts clearer and easier for them to absorb and understand and finally put into use and score lots of marks without much endeavor and fear.

Some might feel that I could have included essay and letter in this book but I don't feel the need for that as accoeding to me, if you know that grammar and if you know some vocabulary, you can write any essay or letter and to any length.

If the reader needs clarity kindly write to me on *batugopal.kks@gmail.com*.

Thank you very much

Ingram Content Group UK Ltd.
Milton Keynes UK
UKHW021825250723
425770UK00016B/819